Diary

of a

Shropshire

Lass

JANET BAINES

Diary

of a

Shropshire

Lass

EDITOR
RACHEL - CLAIRE CUNYNGHAME

Published by Loose Chippings Books
The Paddocks
Chipping Campden
Gloucestershire
GL55 6AU
www.loosechippings.org

Printed and bound in England

ISBN 978-0-9554217-3-0

FOREWORD

This book has been written to celebrate the 90th Birthday of Janet Douglas Baines (née Ward) and also to tell the story of one lady's life from just after the First World War until the present day; a time of great change and upheaval.

It may be difficult for the present generation of youngsters to imagine life without television, let alone iPods and MP3 players. How did people write and find out facts without computers? How did they get around without motor cars? I cannot promise that this book will answer all these questions as it is merely a glimpse of one person's life through the huge changes which took place during the Twentieth Century.

This book is also for Janet's grandchildren, so that they might know some of their family's history.

Rachel-Claire Cunynghame
March 2008

CONTENTS

GROWING UP
IN THE AFTERMATH OF
THE FIRST WORLD WAR

I was born in March 1918 as the First World War came to an end. The world had changed a great deal in those four years since 1914. So many men had been killed during the terrible trench warfare. England was a different place.

There was a move towards female suffrage with the 1918 Representation of the People Act. Only women of property aged over 30 were given the right to vote – not all women, therefore, could vote – but it was a start. The majority of males aged over 21 had been able to vote since 1884, so women were really lagging behind. During the war Britain had experienced a potentially disastrous munitions shortage and this was only solved by women working in the munitions factories. Women also worked in surface jobs on coal mines, drove buses and worked on the land to provide vital food supplies. After the war women were made redundant and expected to regain their pre-war roles; mainly domestic work. Perhaps in fear of a return to the pre-war violence perpetrated by the Suffragist movements, the 1918 act was passed with a huge majority. It was not until 1928 that women achieved full equality of suffrage.

I arrived into the world in the peaceful Shropshire countryside at Shushions Manor, near Wheaton Aston. Shushions had been given to my parents, Richard Pedley Ward and Gertrude (née James) by Gertrude's bachelor uncle, Ben James. The Manor had been in the James family for several generations since 1835. Both my parents' families had been farmers for as long as anyone could remember.

I was the third child after Benjamin and Ruth.

My parents had hoped I would be a boy, which is why my middle name is Douglas! When I was two my father retired from farming and we moved to Weeping Cross House near Stafford where our younger sister, Deborah, was born. The house had been built in the middle of the 19th century by the Twigg family. The house stood for a mere 100 years as it was demolished after my father's death in 1965 to make way for a housing estate. Weeping Cross House was a typical Victorian red-brick building with a glass-domed roof above the hall. We had a cook and a maid who wore uniforms and lived on the top floor of the house.

We did not have mains electricity in those days but we generated our own, which was stored in rows of batteries in an outhouse. There was neither a washing machine nor a fridge; perishables were kept in the cool cellar beneath the kitchen and the laundry took a great deal of time and effort. Today it is strange to think of an era when a constant supply of electricity was not available to everyone. In 1915 the Electric Power

Supply Committee was established which made a recommendation to divide the country into district boards. These boards would take over power generation and distribution in their area. With the Electricity Supply Act of 1925 came the Central Electricity Board which established the National Grid System, linking the biggest power stations across the country and supplying power to existing undertakings. Most of the power was being used by industry but, by 1936, over 12,000 domestic premises had been connected with the help of an assisted wiring scheme.

Weeping Cross House was a good place to grow up, with farmland all around, a grass tennis court and a large kitchen garden where I learnt a great deal from the gardeners; my earliest memories are of washing the clay pots. I think we all inherited a love of gardens from our mother. There were grapes and other fruit in the greenhouses and numerous nut trees in the grounds. Attached to the side of the house a tall conservatory housed Camellias. I still love the waxy beauty of these flowers. In the entrance hall stood a stuffed kangaroo holding a dinner gong (later he was to reside in the walled garden). Our Uncle Ben had brought the creature back from Australia. There were 100 acres at Weeping Cross, most of which was let out to a neighbouring farmer. However, although my father had retired from farming, he still kept a few cattle which he bought in the spring and sold in the autumn after they were fattened. Ruth remembered walking the cattle to market whilst wearing her brother's rather too large boots. We also had a few milking cows for the house; and hens, which ran free in the nut walk surrounding the walled garden; and pigs. My father also ran the shoot at Ingestre Hall; mainly for the South African branch of the family. We used to go along sometimes and enjoyed helping the keepers with the young pheasants. Mother would put on delicious shoot lunches in the outbuildings of Ingestre Hall.

Weeping Cross was part of the Parish of Berkswich which also included Radford, Walton and Milford. Berkswich and Walton are mentioned in the Doomsday Book. Weeping

Cross is thought to have been a place of execution – hence the rather tragic name. The Staffordshire and Worcestershire Canal, which was opened in 1772, ran through our land; it was clean enough for us to swim in! The first railway to run through the parish was opened in 1805 with the main line being opened in 1847. Staffordshire was an important salt and coal producing area. During the 19th century boot and shoe making became a huge industry with some 5 million shoes being shipped out to South Africa alone. The 20th century saw a decline in shoe-making in favour of electronics; GEC being a major employer in the town to this very day.

When Debbie and I were very small (about two and four and dressed in our blue and white striped rompers) we were in the nursery where a fire was burning in the grate. There was a large fire guard around it but Debbie and I were still able to throw our books and toys onto the fire. A lovely blaze ensued but luckily someone smelt fire and came up to put it out – we could easily have burnt the house down! Debbie was very like our mother with her beautiful auburn curls, kindness and generosity. The biggest thrashing I remember was when our father caught Debbie and I dancing on the top of his beloved billiard table!

We three girls all went to Green Hall Preparatory School in Stafford. We had to walk the two miles into Stafford. It was quite good fun because we would pick up our friends on the way. A small grey bus eventually started running; the journey cost 1½d each way. The Misses McCrea, Williams, Moncur and Edger taught us but the best part was playing 'Hide and Seek' in the large gardens. There was a little shop in Rickerscote, on the way back from school, where we would spend our 3d pocket money (a silver threepenny piece = 1¼ decimal pence – would be worth about 50p today)

We had a wonderful nanny called Far (Miss Farrier) who stayed with the family for 56 years until my father's death. She was an absolute saviour to us, as life was rather strict in those days. I certainly spent more time at the top of the house in the nursery and servants quarters than I did with my parents. If we did not eat ALL of the food on our plates we were punished by being sent down into the cellar. My children and grand-children know only too well what a 'Grand Dad plate' means – everything eaten!

There was a Brownie pack at Walton Bury to which I went for a while. We wore brown dresses with a belt, a yellow tie, and a small round straw hat. Miss Allsopp was our Brown Owl and I was in the Fuchsia Six. There was also Miss Tagg's Sunday School to attend in Walton School at 2.00pm on Sunday afternoons. We then went on to the 3.00pm children's service in Walton Church. Leonard Birch was the curate at sometime during the late 20's or early 30's. I, aged about 12, thought he was absolutely marvellous and developed quite a crush on him. How surprised I was to find him turn up again in my life when I was married and went to live in Worcestershire. He was the vicar of Hanbury and baptised our first two children.

In the summer we used to camp out in a large ex-army bell tent. Tennis parties were a common occurrence with all the local boys and girls coming to join in the fun. Our father was a very good left-handed sportsman and, having played tennis at county level, he could easily out-play us three girls on the tennis court. He was also a keen golfer and followed the football at Wolverhampton Wanderers with great enthusiasm. There was a stone-built summer house in the grounds which is where we held meetings of our 'club' – members consisted of: Elma Carnegie (Lake), Doreen Butler (who took slimming pills and nearly died), Mary Youngmark, Stella Tomkinson, Peggy Miller (Pope) and we three girls. We used to put on little plays for both entertainment and to raise funds for Dr. Barnardos. I ran a small library for my friends, encouraged by my mother.

Our nanny, Far, took us for long walks; along the canal and up to Brocton and Cannock Chase.

We were never allowed to return from our walks without bringing back firewood – known as 'sticking'. Mother took us away on holiday to the seaside most years but our father never came with us; I don't think he really liked children! My mother did not learn to drive until the mid 30's when she inherited a car from Granny James. We then all learnt to drive the Austin 12 around the field in front of the house.

I was only eight when the General Strike occurred in 1926, but I do remember Father driving a post office van.

Ben (born in 1910) went to Wolverhampton Grammar School as a weekly border from a young age until he went into farming aged 16. He went to farm at Donnington Wood where Uncle Ted James farmed. When war came Donnington Wood was requisitioned by the Woolwich Arsenal as an Ordnance Depot which it still is to this day. With the compensation, Ben was able to rent the bigger farm of Grindle, near Shifnal in Shropshire, on the Apley Estate, which he farmed for nearly 50 years until his death in 1988. Ben married a Wellington girl, Margaret Smith, known as Pegs, who was a gifted musician. Our father did not really think Pegs would make a good farmer's wife, and even refused to attend their wedding, but he was proved well and truly wrong as they were very happily married for more than 50 years. They had three children; Meyrick, Janice and Gaynor. Horses were still being used on the land well into the 1960's; mainly because Ben really liked the horses.

During the Second World War Ben advised other farmers on the methods to be used for ploughing up land which had never been ploughed; food production was of utmost importance and every scrap of land had to be used. Ben was a very public-spirited person, giving his time to many causes. He was on the Shifnal and Bridgenorth council for some years, chaired the Shropshire National Farmers' Union in 1962 and was awarded an MBE. for his work at the East Shropshire Water Board. Ben's son, Meyrick, took on the tenancy of Grindle after his father's death.

Ruth (born in 1913) went on to Cheltenham Ladies College, where our mother had been educated, whilst Debbie & I went firstly to Stafford High School and then to Howell's School in Denbigh (this was probably because the air was deemed to be better there than in Cheltenham and I was rather a sickly child). Our mother had inherited money from her family by then and it was she who paid our school fees – our father refused to pay as he did not approve of education for girls! I remember Ruth nearly dying of measles and our mother having to sponge her down to reduce her temperature. Our doctor, Dr. Reed, went on his rounds in a pony and trap. He took out my tonsils whilst I lay on the washstand in the spare room (both the wash stand & I survive to this very day).

When Debbie and I were at boarding school our lovely Uncle Ben James, who lived at Upton Hall in Northamptonshire, would send us boxes of snowdrops which he had picked. We were especially thrilled at Christmas when we would find a 10/- (ten shilling) note, from Uncle Ben, on the tree, for each of us. We were very grateful to Uncle Ben as it is he who had financed my father when he started farming and he had also paid Ruth's school fees. We all adored Uncle Ben and felt sad that he did not have his own family, but later on I was glad to hear that he had had a French girlfriend.

I do not remember much about academic matters at school – was this me or the school I wonder? Girls' education was not what it is today. Not many of us were destined for university so, as long as we had a good basic education and were reasonably accomplished in things domestic, we were alright. I did not actually complete my education as I left after General Certificate and before Higher Certificate. I was very keen on both art and games. Howell's had a large shed containing full-size weaving looms, a good art room and a domestic science room. We played lacrosse, tennis, cricket and swam. Unusually the school had a run-down house nearby which we then 'did-up'. This is where I learnt how to plaster walls – a skill which would be very useful in later life. I also enjoyed acting and can still recall some of the productions we put on. I even toyed with going to drama school. When we were away at school we did not come home at all during the term, as it was a long journey for the few days of half-term. We were happy to stay at school with a skeleton staff.

Our Uncle Charles James lived in South Africa and five of his seven children came over to school in England. The journey home was a six-week round trip by boat so they usually stayed with us or other relations during the holidays. It was always fun to have our South African cousins around. Every other year their parents would come over and rent a large house locally, staying for six months.

In 1932, when I was 14, I went to Stratford-upon-Avon with my mother for the opening of the new Shakespeare Memorial Theatre. The theatre had been built incorporating the ruins of the previous theatre (built in 1879) which had burnt down in 1926. It is interesting to note that the Royal Shakespeare Theatre is again being re-built, retaining the 1930's façade, and due to re-open in 2010.

STUDENT DAYS IN ENGLAND, SOUTH AFRICA, AUSTRIA AND GERMANY

We owned two cottages over the road from our house; one was always lived in by the gardener (William, then the Uptons then Fred and Alice Snape). We got to know the inhabitant of the second cottage; a Mrs. Nancy Gardner. 'Mrs. G.', with her cheerful disposition, became our greatest friend and advisor. Later on she moved to a larger house and took in lodgers. As we grew up these men were of great interest to us girls, and my sister Ruth ended up marrying one of them. Mrs. G. always told us that "The apple at the top of the tree is the sweetest"; one of the many proverbs on which we were brought up.

Ruth trained as a teacher at Liverpool Physical Training College (she played lacrosse for the North of England) and went to teach in Newcastle upon Tyne. She had already met Francis Stokes, who was doing his engineering pupillage in Stafford, but she became engaged to another man and was due to go and live in Argentina. When Fanny heard this he rushed up north to claim his 'lost love'. They were married in Holy Trinity Church, Berkswich in 1936 and, after a few months near London, went out to Hong Kong where Fanny was a civilian Civil Engineer attached to the British Navy. In 1939 Ruth gave birth to a son, Timothy, who had Spina Bifida and sadly died a week later. After travelling overland via Saigon to Bangkok they were evacuated by British warship. War was declared whilst they were on the ship and they ended up in South Africa, where they stayed until 1961. By then they had one adopted daughter, Wendy, and three more of their own children, Rosalind, Nigel and Merrilyn.

After leaving school aged 17 in the summer of

1935, I went to Radbrook Domestic Science College in Shrewsbury. During my first term, my mother became very ill, probably with a menopausal breakdown. She spent some months in Northampton Psychiatric Hospital which was a shock to us all. I had to leave Radbrook to help my mother when she returned home. Whilst she was convalescing my father and I took her on a trip to visit her brothers in South Africa. Before we left England I drove Mother over to Wellington to see her solicitor. She wanted to change her will in favour of us children and cut Father out! This was just as well; had she not taken this course of action we would never have seen a penny of her inheritance. It gave us some independence from our father and I was able to pay my own way through college.

The three of us left Tilbury Docks on 19th March 1936 travelling on the 'Llandovery Castle' arriving in Durban on 28th April – no long-haul air flights in those days. Our voyage took us past Tangier and Gibraltar; stopping off at Mallorca.

25th March 1936 - Mallorca

It was a beautiful sunny morning when we anchored in the harbour and the small port couldn't have looked more lovely. On one side the castle, which has lately been restored, stands on a hill, high above the town and surrounded with trees and a deep gorge on either side. The road up to the castle is rough and very dangerous, but the Spanish drivers have no fear, and we thought our end had come many times before we reached the top. After crossing the bridge over the moat we found ourselves in a circular courtyard with an old well in the centre and two tiers of cloisters all round. We had a guide with us who took us up a spiral staircase to the small tower at the top, from which we had a wonderful view of the surrounding country. It was too marvellous to describe because the day was so clear and sunny that it made everything look much more beautiful - the harbour with its masses of fishing smacks and sailing boats; the sea beyond; a long range of blue mountains in the background with tree-covered and rocky foothills descending into deep chasms and valleys where small white villages could be seen, sheltered from the high winds.

Marseilles
Mallorca
Gibraltar
Madeira
Tangier
Port Said &
Suez Canal
Port Sudan
Aden
Zanzibar
Mozambique
Beira
Lourenço
Marques
Durban
Cape Town

My route to and from Africa 1936

After this short stop we were off to Marseilles, we passed through the Straits of Bonifacio, between Corsica and Sardinia, before going through the Suez Canal.

2nd April 1936

Got up at 5.30am so that I shouldn't miss any of the Suez Canal and was just in time to see a war memorial standing out against the morning sky. Dawn was breaking with a red light over the desert and not a sound could be heard, other than the gentle lapping of the water as the ship sailed smoothly on. We passed a few stationary sailing boats whose owners were snoozing quite peacefully and one or two green oases along the banks.

The canal is a wonderful piece of human construction because they had to overcome the great difficulty of sand falling in from the side and blocking up the passage; but both banks are solidly bricked to prevent this and dredgers are constantly at work. We passed through two fairly large natural lakes where ships can speed up for a short time; the limit of the actual canal is 5 mph, and the length about 100 miles. We could see the Italian troop ship in front of us the whole time but otherwise we saw no large craft. There were many camels plodding along in the desert, loaded with goods and others tethered outside the Arab tents.

We had a brief, four-hour stop at Aden and then on to Zanzibar which was amazing. I can still remember the heady aromas of the spices in the market and seeing palm and clove trees for the first time. It was all so very exotic.

17th April 1936 - Zanzibar
We went ashore about 9.30am and toured round the
island in a taxi, going through the clove and coconut
groves to the ruins of the old Sultan's palace; and
coming back through banana plantations where I
tasted my first pink banana – believe it or not! We
explored the shops again and could hardly drag
ourselves away. We sailed about 12 noon.
Total nautical miles run so far: 6795

We stopped again in Mozambique, Beira and
Lorenzo Marques (now Maputo) before arriving
at Durban. We were met by my mother's brother,
Uncle Charles James, and his wife, Aunt Mabel.
It was great fun to meet up with so many of my
cousins. The family had organised a wonderful
itinerary for us visiting all the best places like
Kruger National Park and Victoria Falls; but
when we got up to Johannesburg my mother
had a bad relapse, becoming very depressed and
disorientated. Naturally it was a very distressing
time for both my father and I. She had to go into
hospital but my father and I carried on alone, as
the trip had been planned. We saw Victoria Falls

My grandmother Christiana Ward

My father Richard Pedley Ward

My mother Gertrude, Brother Ben
and Granny Mary James

Weeping Cross House, Stafford, where I grew up

William the gardener

Debbie and I circa 1923

Janet, Ben, Ruth and Debbie
circa 1929

Ruth, Elma, Far, Marjorie and I
1929

Far circa 1930

Uncle Ben James

My father, R P Ward

Me (top left) at Girl Guide Camp 1929

Ben Ward

Ruth Ward

Janet Ward

Debbie Ward

Me on the Llandovery Castle
March 1936

Coaling the ship

Sudanese with camels

Gertrude and R P Ward

Gertrude in Zanzibar 1936

Me in Austria 1937

The Reitter's house in Salzburg 1937
Riedenburgerstrasse 8

Fire Drill 1940
Debbie and I

WER EIN VOLK RETTEN WILL
KANN NUR HEROISCH DENKEN

Hitler Youth near Munich
September 1937

Newcastle Royal Infirmary 1943
I am top left

Newly qualified 1943

Janet, Peggy McDonald and Beryl Jeavons

In Physiotherapy Service uniform

On the move

in the days when the area was so unspoilt. The train was a narrow gauge affair and on the steep gradients we would get out and walk alongside. On the way we stopped off to see the Rhodes Memorial. The Victoria Falls Hotel was the only hotel at the falls and it was fabulous; the food and service impeccable.

A week later, on our return to Johannesburg, we found Mother in a state of collapse. She was rather overweight and this, combined with Johannesburg's high altitude and her already weak condition, brought on heart failure. She died a few days later. She was only 56 and her death was a great shock and very traumatic. She was buried there in Brickston Cemetery, Johannesburg.

On our rather sad journey home without Mother, we took the train down to Cape Town, where we boarded the 'Warwick Castle'. We had Uncle Charles and Aunt Mabel and a couple of the cousins (Betty and Pooh) for company. This voyage took us up the west coast of Africa with a stopover in Madeira.

The voyages to Africa and back were both interesting and fun as we met so many different people and saw all those exotic places. I think it was this expedition which whetted my appetite for travel. I have certainly always been drawn back to Africa.

It was a sad home-coming and especially difficult for our father as he had had little to do with our up-bringing. My sister Ruth's wedding had been arranged for the August and this went ahead. Debbie and I were bridesmaids. Mother had told Ruth to buy her trousseau whilst we were away but, on our return, Father made her take everything back except her wedding dress. I think I rather malign my father; he had some good attributes and if he had had more education (he left school aged 14) he might have had a more rounded character. He didn't exactly do badly as he was able to retire from farming aged 39 and then played the stock market rather successfully; he had some sort of innate intuition where financial dealings were concerned. He also taught us all to play bridge, for which I am eternally grateful; but he was rather lacking in kindness and generosity. He also suffered from gout which might not have helped his disposition. We certainly learnt some thriftiness from our father. In those days used cheques were returned by the bank and he would keep them neatly folded, like a spill, in a pot on the mantelpiece, to be used to light his pipe. The Financial Times had a second life – neatly cut into squares and threaded onto string to hang by 'the throne' (the loo).

After my mother died I was at a loose end, so I went to help out with a family called Henshaw in nearby Brocton. Sam Henshaw was a golfing friend of my father. One bizarre thing I do remember is that Sam ate rice pudding every day.

By late 1936 I wasn't sure what to do but, through a friend, I had an introduction to a family in Salzburg. I went to stay with the Reitter family in return for teaching their daughter English.

7th December 1936
Dad, Mr. Marshall and I left Dover at 11.45am -
terrible crossing and felt violently sick, and was! Got
to Ostend at 3.30pm and took train to Cologne - about
5 hours. The manager of the hotel spoke English
fluently and was awfully friendly and nice. The beds
had no blankets but eiderdowns sewn into a sheet.

We continued by train to Munich and then on to Salzburg where we were met by Frau Reitter. My father and Mr. M. went on to Vienna for a few days holiday before returning to England to the national scandal caused by the King's abdication on 10th December. This had been brewing for some time but it was nonetheless a shock to hear it on the radio in Austria. He had chosen to marry Mrs. Simpson, a divorcee, rather than follow his duty as King. On 14th December the by now ex King, Edward, stayed a night in Salzburg on his way to Vienna.

Salzburg was a lovely place to be; so much music

and beautiful architecture. I learnt to ski for the first time, as well as really enjoying the country and its people. Dr. Reitter was a lawyer and I met many influential people there including the Von Trapp family.

I was asked to leave the house in April 1937 but was not quite sure why. I only found out later that Goebbels and Goering sometimes visited the Reitter's house in Salzburg to discuss the future of Austria. Dr. Reitter later became the local gauleiter – the title given to the Nazi party leader in a particular area. The gauleiters were, in practice, the unquestionable rulers of their particular areas of responsibility. Obviously my hosts did not deem it sensible to have an English girl in the house! I went to stay with a dentist's family and every morning I went to the Hotel Europa to talk English with Herr Jung who ran the hotel. We would have breakfast in the garden and sometimes played tennis.

I suppose a girl of my age should have been thinking of returning home but I was enjoying myself and did not feel threatened. I then spent four months in Munich, at first with the widow of a brownshirt (German storm trooper) who had a daughter of marriageable age. The only problem being that I seemed more attractive to all the young men who came to the house, so I was not very popular with the mother! I went off and found digs elsewhere and attended the Deutsche Acadamie to learn German properly. I had fun and met many young people. I fell madly in love with Wolfgang Wagner, one of my professors, who wanted to marry me. By the autumn of 1937 I realised that I did not want to change my nationality and become embroiled in another country's politics so called it off and went home. It was certainly a most interesting time for me to have been living there.

Austria was a very poor country. The Austro-Hungarian Empire was divided up after the First World War and Vienna was left with too little land to make it viable. They had to decide whether to go with Germany or Italy.

On 12th March 1938 the Anschluss took place. This was the annexation of Austria into Greater Germany by the Nazi regime. There had been pressure to unify the German populations of Austria and Germany prior to this date. Germany had provided support for the Austrian National Socialist Party in its bid to seize power from Austria's leadership. A well-planned internal overthrow of Austria's state institutions took place in Vienna on 11th March. With power quickly transferred over to Germany, the Wehrmacht troops entered Austria to enforce the Anschluss. No fighting took place and the strongest voices against the annexation, particularly Fascist Italy, France and the United Kingdom (the "Stresa Front"), were powerless or, in the case of Italy, appeased. The Allies were, on paper, committed to upholding the terms of the Treaty of Versailles, which specifically prohibited the union of Austria and Germany.

The Anschluss was one of the first major steps in Adolf Hitler's long-desired creation of an empire; to include all the German-speaking lands and territories which Germany had lost after the First World War. Prior to the 1938 annexation, the Rhineland had been retaken and the Saar region had been returned to Germany after 15 years of occupation. After the Anschluss, the predominantly German Sudetenland of Czechoslovakia was taken, with the rest of the country becoming a protectorate of Germany in 1939. That same year, Memelland was returned from Lithuania, the final event and antecedent before the invasion of Poland, which prompted the Second World War.

Back in England, I was playing golf one day with my friend Molly Thorpe who suggested that I might train as a physiotherapist. I did not have the right qualifications for the course but I secured an interview and was offered a place at Newcastle Royal Infirmary; so I went up there in 1939 to train. I cannot remember what the fees were but it did cost me £30 a week for my board and lodging. I thoroughly enjoyed being in the North-East; the people were kind and the golf courses great to play.

Whilst I was training, my father, my sister Debbie and Far had a really bad car accident – on one of those three-lane roads which, ever since then, I have called 'my side, your side and suicide'. Debbie sustained a knee injury which meant she could not take up her job as a matron in an evacuated school in Sidmouth, Devon. So, in my second year, I gave up my training to take up her place for a few months.

I went back to my training, having missed a term and qualified after three years. By then I had bought myself a second-hand Austin Seven for £5. I had to tickle the carburettor to get it running but it took me safely up to Newcastle and back. Although driving tests were introduced in 1935 they were then suspended for the duration of the war and resumed in 1946 so I never had to take one.

With the imports of food declining because of German U-Boat attacks on shipping and the advance of the German army across Europe, food shortages developed in Britain. A rationing system was started but was very complex, as products went onto ration at different times and in different ways. Butter, bacon and sugar were the first foods to be rationed in January 1940. They were followed by meat and preserves in March and so on until just about everything was rationed. Ration books were issued and householders had to register at their local shop. Everything was very strictly controlled, including the prices charged and the quantities supplied. There was, of course, quite a lot of fraud and a black market. People who lived in the countryside were better off because they could probably find some land to grow extra vegetables and fruit and, maybe, keep some chickens or a pig.

The benefit of this system, with a national loaf made of whole-wheat and the restricted intake of sugar and fat, was that the population actually became healthier; they might have been thinner but the natural death rate fell. After the end of the war better supplies of food gradually came back in. Rationing was still in place in 1954 for meat, bacon, butter and cheese. It took a long time for the country to get back on its feet.

The main methods for communicating to the population were the radio and newspapers. BBC radio broadcasts were used to keep everyone aware of what was going on both abroad and in this country. There were televisions by then but they were very expensive (costing about £100 – the same price as a small car!) and could only function within a 40 mile radius of Alexandra Palace. Television broadcasts ceased altogether during the war and did not resume until 1946. It was not until the Coronation of Elizabeth II in June 1953 that televisions became more usual and, even then, the picture was in black and white – colour televisions were introduced in 1967.

Being a farmer, my brother, Ben, was in a reserved occupation, exempting him from military service, and continued to farm at Grindle. In Newcastle I introduced my younger sister, Debbie, to Morton Douglas and they married in Glasgow in 1940. Debbie and I went to the White House department store in London to buy Debbie's trousseau. Whilst we were there I thought I would also buy some sheets and towels. The assistant asked me what name would I like embroidered on the items. I replied that I had not actually found a husband yet but could they keep the goods until such time as I would need them? After the war, when I had found a husband, I was relieved to find that the goods were still in store, and I was able to take possession of my lovely Egyptian cotton sheets and towels which did service for many years. Debbie was in the WRNS for a while until she had her first child. Later on, with their three children, Michael, Gavin and Helen, they lived in Bath and Kent before returning to Staffordshire when Morton retired from the navy.

By the time I qualified as a physiotherapist in 1943, aged 25, the Second World War was already well under way (it began in September 1939). I went to work for a short time in an emergency

44

hospital in Sedgefield, County Durham and then, being young and adventurous, I joined the Overseas Physiotherapy Service.

Whilst waiting for a posting I worked at Addenbrooke's Hospital in Cambridge, where I had a very lively time. I lived with a kind family in Little St. Mary's Lane.

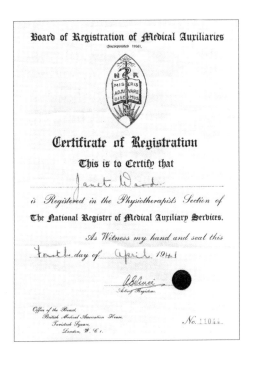

WAR!
REHABILITATING THE WOUNDED

In November 1943 I was called up and made my way to Aldershot to meet the rest of my detachment. In the Overseas Physiotherapy Service we were attached to the army with officer status but wore Red Cross uniform and were under the auspices of the Red Cross. This arrangement turned out to be advantageous as we were under the command of the Colonel rather than the Matron!

We left by troop train in November 1943; complete with tin trunk, bedding roll, canvas wash stand, camp bed, bucket and topi (some of these items are still in existence!) I palled up with Beryl Jeavons and Peggy McDonald who remained firm friends and we managed to stay together for most of our time overseas. Our secret destination turned out to be Greenock in Scotland where a convey was forming. Our ship was an ex passenger liner and full of troops, army nurses and about 12 of us physios. It was pretty basic but, as you can imagine, we had a lot of fun. We didn't have a clue where we were going and sailed quite a way out into the Atlantic to avoid German U-Boats before turning sharply east for Gibraltar. We were escorted by destroyers and a submarine – I think we only lost one ship and picked up the survivors – before landing in Algiers, North Africa, just before Christmas.

We were taken in army vehicles along the coast to Chenova, just west of Tipaza, where we were put into holiday villas attached to an army officer's convalescent depot (the 67th General Hospital). I can still remember the smell of mimosa and wild narcissus which grew abundantly. You can imagine how welcome we were to all these sex-starved & homesick men! It was a wonderful time and we made many good friends; Stephen Hoare and Tony Duveen in particular – both in tank regiments and wounded in the desert. They recovered from their injuries and went back to their regiment but, sadly, Stephen died fighting during the battle at Lake Tresimeno in Italy. Later, I found his grave and took photographs to show his mother in Surrey after the war; a very brave lady. It was very difficult not getting emotionally involved with our patients, particularly knowing that they would be going back to the front.

After Christmas Peggy, Beryl and I were posted to the 100th Hospital at Philipville further east along the coast. We had to travel in an ambulance train, in a coach marked '20 Hommes ou 6 Cheveaux'. It took about two days to reach our destination, sitting on our bed rolls if I remember rightly. When we eventually arrived at our army hospital we found that they had just had a big storm, which had blown down the tented hospital and Matron was not at all pleased to see us – more people to house and feed. The bushes all around were covered with clothes and linen drying in the sun. A row of large holiday villas along the coast was commandeered. Matron was installed in the Sultan's villa and we were in the harem buildings behind – two to a room. The marquees were quickly re-erected and work began. Imagine our horror to find the latrines were five holes in a row with no privacy at all – everybody puffing away on their cigarettes as they did their business!

The casualties were coming in from the North African Campaign even though Rommel had just about caved in and most of the action had moved on to Italy. It was our job to get the men fit enough to rejoin their units or, if too badly injured, to get them well enough to travel home in hospital ships. Douglas Bader was always an inspiration to the men. Bader might have lost his legs in a flying accident before the war, but the very fact that he was able to fly (rather well) with two prosthetic legs was great motivation and made the men realise that there was hope for them even if they were badly injured.

Throughout the war my father and Far took in evacuees from various parts of the country. I remember that, at one stage, Ramsgate was evacuated to Stafford and two teachers went to stay at Weeping Cross; Father and Far thoroughly enjoyed their company. My father was always a great letter-writer and throughout the war wrote to me and was always keen to hear my news. I have been searching for the letters which I wrote home to him but can only find oddments. I did find my posting order to the 100th General Hospital in Philipville by the ambulance train.

Copy.   Re - Posting.   29 · 12 · 43.

1.   Miss WARD :   } to :-
     Miss McDONALD :   }

          No. 100 General Hospital
                    Philippeville.

2.   Authority :- A.F.H.Q letter
          Pay. Mis 4 (a) dated
                         24 - 12 - 43.

3.   You will travel on the
     Ambulance Train 88 21
     departing Central Station,
     Algiers at 1805 hours.
     1 Jan. 44. Transport
     will report to 'A' Officers

51

My overseas service
November 1943 to August 1948

1939 - 1943	PhysiotherepyTraining at Newcastle Infirmary
November 1943	Leave Greenock, Scotland
December 1943	Arrive Chenova, Algeria
January 1944	Philipville
February 1944	El Biar, Algiers
March 1944	Naples
May 1945	Ghent, Belgium
June 1945	Rendsburg, Germany
Early 1946	Osnabrück
March 1946	Münster
February 1947	Klagenfurt, Austria
August 1948	Home to be married

I also found some love letters from Tony Duveen – I don't remember being in love with him but I do remember him tracking us down in Philipville and climbing through our window one evening (he didn't let on that he was already married!) In those days we were all jolly good friends and NO SEX! Where we lived at that time was right on the beach at Philipville and we had lovely bathing, even though it was winter.

After a month, Philipville hospital was closed and we were sent back to the 94th Hospital at El Biar near Algiers, where there were four military hospitals; all tented. We were lucky to be able to explore the town as it soon became 'off limits'. The Arab quarter, the kasbah, was the most interesting but we did not go un-escorted. We were close to the coast and one day went down to bathe. When we emerged from the water we found that some Arab scoundrel had stolen our clothes so we had to return to the hospital dressed only in our bathing suits. They even got into the compound one night and stole everything out of one of the girls' tents – even her camp bed – without her being disturbed! We were six physios in all and we palled up with the physiotherapy department of the convalescent depot at Tipaza on the coast. Betty Lloyd was one of these and we have remained friends ever since.

In 1944, after about 6 months, we were on the move again; this time over the sea to Naples (67th General Hospital) where the battle was raging at Monte Cassino. This was a costly series of four battles fought by the Allies (British, American, French, New Zealanders and Polish) with the intention of breaking the German Winter Line and seizing Rome. In February 1944 the historic abbey of Monte Cassino, sitting high on a peak overlooking the town, was destroyed by American bombers. The bombing was based on the fear that the Germans were using the site as a look-out post for the Axis defenders. At the time they were not, but two days after the bombing German troops poured into the ruins to defend it.

A great many of our patients were in a bad way with lost limbs and were waiting for hospital ships to take them home. The 67th Hospital was in a deserted school, in the slum area near the port of Naples. We slept in dormitories of ten to a room with our goods and chattels stacked up around us. During the winter months it was very cold. Our department was in the basement which was rather dark. We constructed a little oven out of a paraffin stove and a large biscuit tin so that we could make more of our rations. The street outside was used as a latrine by the locals who just came and squatted to relieve themselves, which was rather disgusting. I remember being quite surprised to see that the local cemetery was full of expensive marble tombs; I think people spent more money on their tombs than on their homes.

The wounded would be taken first to dressing stations where their wounds were assessed and patched up as best they could be. They would then be moved away from the front to the hospitals. We had all the bad casualties; broken and shattered limbs, mine wounds, missing limbs etc. We had to try to keep the chaps spirits up as we got them as comfortable as possible. It was grim work but we all felt that we were contributing to the war effort in the best way we could.

The battle for Cassino raged on for a long time; one of our nursing sisters was killed when she was dealing with a casualty up near the front. From January till May the defences were assaulted four times by Allied troops. Finally, after heavy fighting, the Poles captured Monte Cassino on 18th May 1944. These operations resulted in casualties of over 54,000 Allied and 20,000 German soldiers.

The patients and staff were sometimes lucky enough to be entertained with performances by ENSA (Entertainment National Service Association). A wide variety of entertainers spent the war years travelling around the different theatres of war giving concerts and variety performances. They never quite knew where they might end up but they certainly gave an enormous number of people a great deal of pleasure. Whilst I was in Naples, Joyce Grenfell was on tour. We went to watch her one-woman show (Joyce and an accompanying pianist) which was great fun. We were also treated to 'Behold The Man' at the Bellini Theatre.

There was a pleasant side to being where we were. It was an opportunity for us to be in Naples with no tourists; our leave centres were Sorrento, Amalfi, Positano and the island of Ischia where we boiled potatoes in the hot springs. We were able to visit Pompeii and Herculaneum and were in Naples when Vesuvius erupted. Between 13th and 29th March 1944 Vesuvius was active and sadly the villages of San Sebastiano and Massa were engulfed by lava and destroyed. The allies were caught by surprise when the eruption occurred; air force planes were destroyed at the airfield at Terzigno. Hot lava rained down on our flat roof which was rather frightening – I managed to take a piece of lava home – and the surrounding area was covered in grey ash.

We were very popular with the chaps and had a great time on our days off. Ischia was beautiful in those days. It was totally unspoilt; no tourists but there were some cafés and restaurants open which were very happy to welcome us. One of our friends, Barbara Richardson, met her husband-to-be in 'The Orange Grove' nightclub in Naples and, after only six outings, they married in the church at San Pasquale. I am glad to say that they both survived the rest of the war to have a long and happy marriage. I lost so many good friends during those dreadful war years.

9th January 1945
Big German offensive in France. Russians fighting for Budapest.

27th January 1945
Russians only 100 miles from Berlin.

12th February 1945
We heard that we are moving in two weeks. Great celebrations - never have I been so pleased to move anywhere. This place has really got us all down.

12th March 1945
Very busy day working until 6.30pm. German POWs,
lots of Yugoslavs and British Tommies from Greece
and the 8th Army.

We were sent up to Barletta and then recalled to Naples three days later to find that we are being shipped out to Marseilles; the whole hospital was packed up. I told the men not to include our biscuit tin oven but, to my surprise, during the loading, I saw "Little Beattie", as we called it, sitting on top of all the hospital equipment. I don't actually remember being hungry whilst on war work and I am still amazed at how sufficient our food was. It must have been a great logistical operation to keep the supply-lines open. I seem to think that my pay during those years would be equivalent to about £8,000 today.

On our arrival in Marseilles, we slept on 'The Blue Train', in a siding, for two nights before flying to Brussels in a Dakota DC3, for the crossing of the Rhine. We ended up in Ghent in Belgium, before taking over an ex German army hospital; full of starving patients with suppurating wounds covered in paper bandages. As I spoke German it fell to me to do the translating. Most of the patients were glad to be out of it all but I was spat on by one Luftwaffe pilot whom I was treating for leg injuries. The end of the war was now in sight.

7th May 1945 - Ghent
Great expectations for victory. Had dinner with the pathologist in the club where the end of the war was announced. Met some very nice people in the street and finished up with omelettes in the department.

8th May 1945 - Ghent
VE Day. Work as usual. Had a party in the evening, which was good fun. We rode round the town on a jeep.

I went home on leave for a short while before returning to join the hospital in Rendsburg, on the Kiel Canal, for three or four months where we looked after the army of occupation. We took over an army barracks, where one of the buildings was full of German prostitutes; there for the convenience of the German troops. We had to get rid of them and clean the place up. We inherited a whole stable of beautiful ex SS horses and my riding career got underway. I had a beautiful grey horse called Sinbad which I rode out every morning before work. We were not far from the Danish border and our eyes opened wide to see all the goodies in the shops and how clean the country was. The main currency at that time was cigarettes which we could buy from the NAAFI (the forces trading organisation). I managed to trade 1,000 cigarettes for £25 and ended up buying a Copenhagen dinner service, which I somehow managed to ship home – it is still in use.

One of our rather sad jobs was to service train-loads of Belsen 'skeletons' on their way to Sweden to be resuscitated. These were the people who had actually survived the horrific treatment meted out by the Germans in the concentration camps. They were in such appalling condition; emaciated by the lack of food, diseased, poorly dressed and totally dispirited. People in Britain found it difficult to believe the stories which emerged at this time about both the concentration camps and the far worse death camps where millions of Jews and others were killed.

7th August 1945
The disclosure of the atom bomb dropped on Japan.

10th August 1945
The Japs have given unconditional surrender. Isn't it terrific? We celebrated by having a good hour in the riding school and then a marvellous meal of venison at the 77th Mess.

In early 1946 I was posted down to Osnabrück and then on to Münster which had been completely flattened by Allied bombers; but the ex SS hospital (which became the 25th General Hospital) on the outskirts was untouched and we had really good accommodation – I actually had a room to myself. Once again we inherited a stable full of horses and rode out every morning before work. I had not wanted this posting. It was the first time I was separated from Beryl and Peggy, who had left the army and gone home, but it was here that my future would be sealed. By this time wives (and families) were coming out to join their husbands; so we had both male and female patients as well as a maternity wing. Our job was to keep the army of occupation fit.

I was in charge of the physiotherapy department (aged 27) and one day I walked into the duty room of one of the wards to be captivated by a most attractive man with bright blue eyes sitting on the floor. It was literally love at first sight – crashing of cymbals etc. Guy Baines was head surgeon; dying to get home and find a permanent job, but they needed him there pro tem. We got to know one another – I even had to go fishing with his group to catch him – we had a lot in common, apart from the fishing! Neither of us had wanted to marry during the war and so we were a bit older as a result.

Whilst I was in Paris in 1937 a fortune teller had told me of a man with eyes of a lighter blue than

Me taking an exercise class in Naples 1944

On Michael at Lendorf 1947

On leave in Ischia 1944

Beryl, Peggy and I

At Klagenfurt Races 1948

Skiing at Lendorf

Jumping on Strawberry
at Klagenfurt 1948
I won 3rd Prize

Guy and I going fishing
soon after we had met
Munster 1946

Guy and I newly engaged - Italy 1948

Mabel
Baines

Albert
Baines

Guy with apples circa 1920

Guy, Brenda and Roger 1924

Charterhouse
Swimming Team
1930

Guy
(3rd from left)

Guy, Roger, Mabel and Brenda
at Roger's wedding 1940

Guy in the 1930's

Guy in uniform

Our Wedding

30th October 1948

Baswich Church

Near Stafford

Cattespoole 1947

Guy on the Fergie at Cattespoole

mine and fair hair who would be very fond of me but there was a cloud between us at present. Thank goodness the clouds parted!

It might be a surprise to some that Guy designed an evening dress for me which I had made up by a local dressmaker in midnight blue velvet with the button loops fashioned out of parachute cord. Guy was demobbed and returned to the Queen Elizabeth Hospital, in Birmingham, in January 1947, where he had been the first Resident Surgical Officer when it opened in 1936. He was fortunate to get a consultant job straight away.

I was posted down to Klagenfurt, in Austria; we travelled by train but it was the year of the great snow and we were stuck in the train for two days. The winter of 1947 was very long and cold. From 22nd January until 17th March, snow fell every day somewhere in Britain. The temperature seldom rose more than a degree or two above freezing. Food was already in short supply after the years of war and this prolonged winter compounded the problems. The same was true of central Europe with children in Vienna being moved to the wealthier western countries, such as Belgium.

The British Zone of Occupation in Austria was mainly the southern part of Austria including the Eastern Tyrol, Carthinia and Styria. The occupation of Austria lasted for ten years until 1955. I was stationed in Lendorf just outside Klagenfurt; again, a military hospital which was well-equipped (the 31st General Hospital). On our doorstep we had skiing at Lendorf and sailing on the Wörtersee. We inherited German army horses yet again and, in our free-time, had a marvellous time. Guy came out on holiday in 1948 and we went down to Italy for a holiday where he asked me to marry him.

THE MAN I MARRIED
GUY BAINES

Guy would have preferred to have been born in Yorkshire and considered himself to be a Yorkshire man (by parentage) rather than a Lancastrian (by birth).

He was born on 16th September 1911 in St. Helens, Lancashire, the third child of Canon Albert and Mabel Baines (née Harrison). Roger was his elder brother by four years with Brenda, the girl between the two boys. Their parents were somewhat austere but life was happy if rather formal. Guy hated the stiff collars which he had to wear, and having to sit still in church on Sundays; particularly as his father was the vicar! In later life Guy's preferred mode of dress was to wear a loose-fitting short-sleeved shirt with a tie and a rather sloppy suit. For work he wore operating 'greens' so was perfectly comfortable. He always disliked wearing his dinner jacket or morning dress.

When Guy was three an accident occurred in the nursery and a pot of boiling water fell onto him scalding his arm very badly. He was lucky to survive such an injury in a pre-antibiotic era and was left with a large scar.

Guy began his education at Mostyn House School, Cheshire, where he said he learnt, amongst other things, how to stuff birds (the avian type!) sand-yachting, roof-climbing and monotype composition. He moved on to Charterhouse in Surrey where he became head of his house, Verites, and deputy head boy. He avoided classics by doing the only alternative - the sciences, which in turn lead to him studying medicine. In a memoir he said he represented the school at most sports except cricket, old time dancing and knitting! He was especially good at

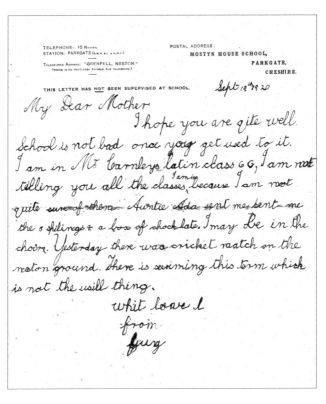

TELEPHONE: 10 Neston.
STATION: PARKGATE (G.R.&L.&N.W.)
TELEGRAPHIC ADDRESS: "GRENFELL, NESTON."
(THERE IS NO PORT/PAID PAYABLE FOR TELEGRAMS)

POSTAL ADDRESS:
MOSTYN HOUSE SCHOOL,
PARKGATE,
CHESHIRE.

THIS LETTER HAS NOT BEEN SUPERVISED AT SCHOOL.   Sept 18th 1920

My Dear Mother
          I hope you are qite well.
School is not bad once you get used to it.
I am in Mr Earnleys latin class 6 G, I am not
telling you all the classes, because I am not
quite sure of them. Auntie Ada sent me sent me
the 5 shilings & a box of chocklate. I may be in the
choir. Yesterday there was cricket match on the
neston ground. There is swimming this term which
is not the usill thing.
               whit love
                    from
                    guy

Guy's first letter home from prep school
Aged just 9

71

swimming and his 100yd freestyle record was not bettered for many years. He was captain of boxing and swimming. Albert Baines was not too enamoured with his son's choice of medicine; he probably thought he should have gone into the church. It was not until years later, when Albert himself was in hospital, that he told Guy that he had, at last, come to understand why he had chosen that particular career.

Guy's elder brother, Roger, was born in Newcastle under Lyme. He also attended Charterhouse, before becoming ordained and spending some years teaching in Uganda. He married Geraldine Mary Gordon Fisher in 1940, and they had three sons: Richard, Martin and Stephen. He spent the greater part of his ministry at St. Peter's Church in Harrogate, becoming a canon of Ripon cathedral in 1956. He took early retirement to serve a clutch of churches in Herefordshire and preached his last sermon at the age of 90! Roger was a talented carpenter and spent much time in his workshop turning out furniture for the home, both decorative and practical. He also loved big machines, particularly trains.

Brenda was rather in awe of her brothers and sometimes felt inferior to them. She need not have done. She was a dutiful daughter who stayed at home to look after both her parents until their deaths. She became a district nurse, and travelled through Yorkshire administering her excellent brand of care to her patients. Brenda was fond of children. She had many clever little ideas for making life for parents easier; particularly a special double knot for shoe laces. Brenda was a staunch Christian and the first lady churchwarden at St. John the Baptist, Knaresborough. She was also a school governor. Brenda, with her companion, Pat Bramley, lived a very busy life. They shared a caravan and then a holiday house in the very north of Scotland, as they were both keen ornithologists. In retirement Brenda took up carpentry and was rather adept at using a lathe for turning wood.

The early Baines family holidays were spent at various seaside resorts; there was certainly a trip to Borth, Wales, in 1922 with their cousins Malcolm and Eleanor Harrison. When the children were teenagers the family would set off for the Alps for their summer holidays. There was a three-week expedition to Austria in July 1936; carefully written up in a diary by Brenda. The group was made up of: Mother and Father Baines with Mother's sister, Alice, a Mr. Hinde, Brenda and Guy. The family visited Innsbruck, Sölden and St. Anton for the walking and climbing. The Baines family were all tall, slender people; well suited to striding across the countryside.

All of the Baines siblings were keen gardeners. In later life Roger grew chrysanthemums with great enthusiasm, along with all the usual garden plants; Brenda kept chickens, bees and grew all manner of fruit and vegetables; whilst Guy ran a large vegetable plot, as well as the farm, to keep his family fed.

Guy worked hard and during his time at St. John's College, Cambridge, he was able to complete his BA and an MB in two years rather than three. He then had time to devote his third year to wider reading in anatomy and physiology and to gaining a valuable start in medicine at Addenbrooke's Hospital. He seems also to have spent time playing all manner of games in and out of the water, boxing ring, rugger field and athletics track as well as Newnham and Girton Colleges and most hostelries! He gained blues for both swimming and boxing, which he apparently took up to overcome his shyness. He was also President of the University Medical Society.

St. Thomas's Hospital in London offered Guy the Hector MacKenzie Exhibition in 1933 (was this for intelligence or prowess on the games field?) Following the usual exams there followed the normal 2½ year stint of house jobs with very little salary. Having been offered a registrar's job in London, he then heard, through the grapevine, that there were going to be jobs coming up in somewhere called Birmingham! Research shewed that it had a lot of advantages

– principally that there was good country on its doorstep. The new Queen Elizabeth Hospital in Edgbaston employed Guy as one of their new surgical registrars under B.J.Ward and Prof. Barling who wouldn't speak to each other, which must have made life a bit difficult. Guy gained his Fellowship in May 1939.

No sooner had Guy got settled in than the Second World War started. All registrars in the Midlands were prevented from joining the military as it was a 'Reception Area' for war casualties; but fairly rapidly his fellow members of staff were dispersed to other hospitals leaving Guy with a huge work-load, and very few staff, to look after 900 beds. Half the wards were set aside for service personnel. Convoys of wounded arrived by train, often in the middle of the night. They were all nationalities: British, Russian, French, Belgian and even Turkish with a few German prisoners-of-war. The civilians were often victims of air raids. All this, together with the day-to-day surgery, provided wonderful experience (at one time Guy had 200 personal beds) BUT the hours were a bit long! They used to reckon on getting to bed at 2.00 am on four nights, 4.00am on two nights and not at all one night in the week.

During these days of rationing he somehow managed to get a splendid cooked breakfast in bed on a Sunday morning – pinched from the kitchens by a sweet little blond! (who, incidentally, ended up in prison after the war). Guy never lost the work ethic and I can remember well how, in later years, after lunch on a Sunday he would allow himself a few minutes to drink a cup of coffee with one or two pieces of chocolate and then he was up and back out onto the farm or garden.

Despite being in a 'retained' occupation, Guy tried three times to join up. He was, eventually, allowed to join the Royal Army Medical Corps in 1943. He was told to go to Leeds, where he was welcomed by one of his old students who was the Commanding Officer. Apparently this was the wrong place so he got kitted up and was sent off to Aldershot. The unit (First Airborne Division) was going to North Africa so he had a crash course in how to parachute – no problems except that later x-rays suggested that a fractured neck was probably acquired here. Then he was off to Algeria where he spent a pretty miserable time waiting to land in Sicily - doing impossible exercises without drinking water. At one stage he did get hold of some water and drank 18 pints in one go!

Alexander Fleming went out to tell the medics about the first antibiotic, penicillin. He had just one dose of a medicine which we take so much for granted to-day. Fleming had discovered penicillin rather accidentally in 1928 and, although he continued his investigations, he was unconvinced that it could be a useful agent in treating infection. It took the chemists Ernst Chain and Edward Abraham to work out how to isolate and concentrate penicillin, which they managed by 1940. The rest of the team at Oxford University experimented in other ways until the antibiotic was finally tested on a human subject in 1941. By 1944 the drug was being used to treat Allied troops and, very probably, influenced the outcome of the war.

Guy worked on for a while in Algiers – at one stage he became Orthopaedic Consultant for the whole of North Africa. He didn't actually get to Sicily as Hermann Goering's armoured division were closing in. Guy's unit was suddenly sent to Taranto on the Italian surrender.

For several reasons of great luck Guy did not get to the boat which was subsequently blown up by mines in Taranto harbour. He lost most of his good friends in this tragedy. When he did land in Italy Guy's progress up Italy was rapid although fuelled by half rations. He said that he cleaned out every lavatory in every town; which stood him in good stead for the farming he would later do (his daughter, Rachel, still relishes a bit of drain-clearing). The only surgery at this stage appears to have been when the Allied ambulances mistakenly got behind the German lines and the Germans asked them to treat their own injured.

Guy's next close shave with death came when he was due to fly with a battalion commander back to Algiers. The plane (nick-named a 'flying coffin') coming to collect them crashed on the way to pick them up; fortunately for Guy not after they had been picked up.

Subsequently Guy was sent to India – he had a 'personal posting' which he took to be some sort of punishment, but for what he did not know. It later transpired that the idea was to raise an Indian Airborne Division, so they had sent out people from each branch of the services. The journey to India involved travelling in one of the beautiful flying boats (usually reserved for Major-Generals and above). Karachi was lousy and Calcutta too near the war, so Guy went up to Delhi – which turned out to be the correct place but no-one had told him that. He had three weeks to see all the sights and was then posted to a hospital on full pay and told not to work! Eventually Guy was told that his 'job' was not ready and what would he like to do? He opted to join a Forward Surgical Unit and had his third lucky escape, as there was no transport. Had he got to where he should have been he would have been slaughtered by the Japanese in the Arakan.

Guy's next lucky escape involved his refusal to travel in the forward 3-tonner driven by an Indian who drove the truck off a long bridge into the Irrawaddy river. Eventually they arrived at their unit which was no more than a hole in the ground surrounded by slit trenches. As they were the only surgical unit on the front they did a lot of work in spite of the really bad administration. The team was kept going by an untouchable, who brewed a pint of tea in a small dark hole between each case in the underground theatre. Conditions were such that sweat just poured out of their boots. A marvellous Quartermaster provided a fine draught of chlorine, orange juice and rum in equal quantities to revive them at the end of the day.

The monsoon came, which was a relief to begin with, but they were then withdrawn before conditions became too bad. The climate affected Guy rather badly; his dicey skin and bullous impetigo stripped the skin from his back (he had nearly been sent home from North Africa twice for the same reason). He returned to England very slowly on a Polish transport ship. They didn't have much to eat but they managed to play bridge for 14 hours a day – Guy was 3d up by the end of the journey. Two weeks leave in Glasgow followed – this was Guy's only leave during the war.

After that Guy was off to the Royal Herbert Hospital in Woolwich – V2 rockets were falling all around causing Guy's windows to be blown in regularly. The first V2 rockets were launched in September 1944 and, over the next six months, more than 3,000 were launched at various targets in France, Belgium, Germany and The Netherlands. 1,358 of these silent rockets were targeted on London. Because the bombs were silent the British government was able, for a while, to hide the fact that the bombs had actually hit anything, thus keeping the Germans in the dark; not knowing whether their weapons were even reaching England. The V2 was developed by Wernher von Braun and Walter Riedel and was the first ballistic missile and the first man-made object to achieve sub-orbital spaceflight. This rocket was the progenitor of all modern spacecraft. Although the V2 was one of the most advanced weapons of the Second World War it was militarily ineffective. It lacked a proximity fuse; it buried itself in the target area before or just as the warhead detonated thus reducing its effectiveness. Nevertheless 7,000 military and civilians were to die with many more being injured. Sadly about 20,000 slave labourers died in the construction of these rockets.

After this Guy was sent to Belgium where he met up with a couple of his chums and was left with a nice case to deal with; only one lower leg visible – head, neck and all other limbs either missing or in plaster, no veins and a marrow drip which wasn't very successful. The departing consultant's final words were, "Not very well but he will be alright"

After a while here Guy had his best experience of how a war should not be run. He was posted to a Forward Surgical Unit 'just up the road' in Meimegen. The only people there when he arrived were part of a Canadian rear guard who fed Guy but would not let him play poker with them - this was a kindness as the stakes were rather high. His unit had moved on so the Canadian's gave him a jeep for him to "nip up to the unit after lunch". Two days later, after avoiding a battle in one town between the police and displaced people, he eventually found his unit in Luneburg at the other end of Germany. Here he was told that he was in the wrong place and sent to Bremen for the last fighting of the war. He had the weird experience of driving (in an armoured car) down a completely silent, mined street not knowing whether it was 'open' or not. He said that it was the same feeling as standing on a snow precipice alone and not knowing if it's going to 'go'.

With the actual war in Europe at an end, Guy was deployed on the unsavoury task of liberating the Concentration Camp at Sandbostel in Lower Saxony. This tragic experience was to mark Guy for the rest of his life; certainly as far as any belief in God was concerned. He was unable to accept man's devastating inhumanity to other men. The camp was over-crowded, even by German standards (8,000 in a camp built for 1,000) and full of typhus. One prisoner, a Polish doctor, wouldn't let the British look after the dying cases in his hut as he said "I am used to it and you are not". Guy's high opinion of the Poles remained with him. Many of the Russian prisoners-of-war were sent back to Russia – sadly most of them to their deaths. Women and girls from the surrounding countryside were recruited to help with washing and shaving the men. The women were extremely shocked that their own army had been so very cruel to these people. A 'human laundry' was set up to disinfect the men and, eventually, blankets and food arrived. The inmates of Sandbostel were so starved that they were unable to digest ordinary food; many died after the camp was liberated due to this terrible starvation as well as the typhus

As if this wasn't enough, Guy's unit was sent down to Belsen where he commanded the hospital. They missed the first ghastly scenes but there was still plenty to shock. Bergen-Belsen had been set up in 1940 as a prisoner-of-war camp. Between then and spring 1942 about 18,000 Russian soldiers died of hunger, cold and disease. In 1942 Bergen-Belsen became a concentration camp and placed under SS command. Men, women and children were held here; many of them Jews, gypsies, Czechs, Poles, anti-Nazi Christians and homosexuals. Anne Frank and her sister both died there in 1945. Large numbers of prisoners were moved to the camp from other camps as the Russians advanced on the eastern front. The number of deaths increased due to disease, particularly typhus, and starvation. Between 1943 and 1945 an estimated 50,000 people died in Bergen-Belsen. On 15th April 1945 the British and Canadians liberated the camp and found 60,000 prisoners inside (the camp was designed to hold about 10,000 inmates) and another 13,000 corpses lying unburied around the camp. The remaining SS personnel were forced to bury the dead and, as a final act of defiance, the last Germans to leave the camp cut the water supply, making the job of treating the inmates even more difficult. After cleansing the remaining inmates and moving them to a nearby Panzer army camp, the Bergen-Belsen camp was burned to the ground. Guy never talked about his time in these camps – he was too deeply shocked by the experience.

Guy's next posting was down to Gottingen to clear the area before the Russians came in. He had many moves over the next few weeks with a memorable visit to a German hospital full of septic amputations dripping pus – no antibiotics. Shortly after this Guy had to give a lecture at Hamburg University on antibiotics – or rather the one antibiotic that existed! He wasn't totally convinced that they actually believed in the existence of this 'wonder drug'.

After the German war had ended the Japanese war continued but that came to an end when the atomic bombs were dropped on Hiroshima and Nagasaki in August 1945. The bombs themselves killed 220,000 people but many more were to die in the years following from injuries and illnesses attributed to exposure to the radiation released by the bombs. Then ensued many miserable months while Guy waited for demobilisation. He had little time for the army regulars who had gained exalted positions he thought they should never have had, and felt his time was being wasted. In October 1945 Guy was promoted to Lieutenant-Colonel and appointed Officer Commanding the 25th General Hospital in Münster. The only good thing about this period was the fishing, shooting and hunting. Apart from a lot of lesser game, he said it eventually produced a very nice wife for him!

Guy was appointed to the staff of the United Birmingham Hospitals in the middle of 1946 but could not take up the post until January 1947. He had six beds at the Queen Elizabeth Hospital and a few at the General Hospital. He was also on the staff of Kidderminster and the Birmingham Children's Hospital during that time but had to earn his keep by doing emergencies at three guineas a time from Tamworth to Tewkesbury. Guy then took on work from Joe Sankey at Dudley. Work at the QE on six beds was a joke. In a couple of years his waiting list had grown to over 300 so he burnt it and started again. There were no repercussions until 15 years later when a GP wrote to ask if it was yet time to do Mrs. X's thyroid. Guy joined Hugh Donovan on his unit and on Hugh's death Ward West 1 officially became the Urological unit, even though it had been that in all but name. Paul Dawson-Edwards and Guy continued together at the QE for many years with Guy retiring in 1977. Guy was one of the first surgeons to perform a urostomy (ileal conduit – surgical creation of an artificial opening for the bladder) for bladder cancer in the 1950's. Guy was a well-respected surgeon whose patients always came first and he only ever operated if it was absolutely necessary.

A few hospital stories:-

One patient was rather obese so Guy sent him home with a flea in his ear and told him that he would not operate until the man had lost some weight. The said patient returned a few months later having lost four stone on a steak and lettuce diet.

A patient returned each year with the same complaint. On being asked what he did at this time of year that he didn't do for the rest of the year, he replied that he ate his way through a field of rhubarb (which contains oxalic acid – not good for the kidneys)

Guy was driving home one night from work in Birmingham. Two men were thumbing a lift, so Guy slowed down and stopped a little way ahead. They didn't make a move, so Guy approached them to ask if they wanted a lift; but they obviously had other intentions. One made a move to hit Guy who retaliated with his (rather well-trained) fist and laid the man out. Next day, when Guy was in work, the sister asked him to go and see a patient with a broken jaw. Guy poked his head through the curtain and saw his assailant and asked the sister to find someone else to attend him!

When Guy returned to work in Birmingham, the National Health Service was about to become a reality. The NHS formally came into being on 5th July 1948. Previously health care had been the preserve of those who could pay for it although there was some provision for people on very low wages – introduced with the National Insurance Act of 1911. General Practitioners and hospitals charged, though sometimes poorer people would be reimbursed. Mentally ill people were locked away in large institutions, not always for their own benefit but to save other people from embarrassment. Conditions were often so bad that many patients became worse not better. Older people who were no longer able to look after themselves also fared badly. Many ended their days in the workhouse – a Victorian institution feared by everyone. Workhouses changed their names to Public Assistance Institutions in 1929, but their character, and the stigma attached to them, remained.

Nowadays we take the NHS for granted but it was a huge undertaking to establish a system where free health care was available to everyone. Sir William Beveridge reported in 1942 that health care was one of the three pre-requisites of a viable social security system. Aneurin Bevan, under Atlee's labour government, pushed through the necessary legislation to create a system where hospital services, family practitioner services (doctors, pharmacists, opticians and dentists) and community-based services were all in one organisation for the first time. The three main principles of the new health service were: that services would be provided free at the point of use, central taxation would fund the service and everyone would be eligible. It was difficult to hold everything together (there were 2,688 hospitals) and it remains so today. Scientists continue to create new, more expensive drugs, operations become more complex, diagnostic testing ever more thorough and so it goes on. Some charges crept back in over time – prescription charges and dental fees in particular. By the seventies Guy couldn't wait to retire. Matrons had been replaced with managers and he was fed up with all the paperwork and bureaucracy. He was there to heal not to push paper around. Has anything changed?

Mr. Richard Pedley Ward

requests the pleasure of
the company of

Mrs Peggy McDonald

at the marriage of his daughter

Janet,

with

Mr. Guy Harrison Baines,

at Baswich Church, Weeping Cross,
on Saturday, October 30th, 1948,
at 2 p.m.,
and afterwards at Weeping Cross House, Stafford.

Weeping Cross House,
   Stafford.

R.S.V.P.

MARRIED LIFE
WITH A SURGEON
AND FARMER

Being the scion of many generations of farmers, the odds were heavily in favour of me marrying a farmer. No doubt I would have done so had the Second World War not intervened. In fact I married a doctor. So there we were on a fine October day in 1948 getting married in Baswich Church. I had found the material for my dress in Italy and had the dress made up in Vienna. I was lucky as rationing was still in force in Britain and I would never have been able to find such beautiful fabric back in England. I was very pleased when our daughter, Rachel-Claire, chose to wear my wedding dress when she was married in 1977. Our bridesmaids were two of my great friends from war days: Phyllis Wallington and Mabs Cheetham with my nephew, Michael Douglas and niece, Gaye Ward, as the young attendants. Sam Davison was Best Man. My father was rather mean and I had to pay for my own wedding including an outfit for Far.

We went off on honeymoon to Devon leaving my brother, Ben, to go to an auction of a house at Tardebigge in Worcestershire, which I had seen advertised in my local paper. I had rung Guy to ask him whether we had to live in Edgbaston. His reply was emphatically "No" and after I had told him the details he realised that it was the same house which his boss, Mr. Scott-Mason, had rented during the war and which Guy had visited then.

Cattespoole had been owned by Mrs. Gilpin-Brown, the last of the Peyton family who had re-built the house way back in 1639-40 and lived in it for the following 300 years. Mrs. G-B did not have the money to modernise the house (it had neither electricity nor running water and a

With Robert 1950

Robert, Guy, Janet and Rachel 1953

Robert and Rachel on Dixie

Rachel and Robert
outside Cattespoole
circa 1956

Rachel 1957

Family
Holidays

Growing up at Cattespoole

Ben and Pegs Ward
Ruth Stokes
Janet Baines
Debbie Douglas
1975

Ward Family gather for Far's 80th birthday

Richard and Edward Cunynghame
with Harrison Baines-Hilton 1993

Guy in 1980

left: Guy and I
at Redditch WI Market
1982

My 80th Birthday in 1998

Sally, Michael, Arthur, Rachel-Claire, Robert, Jilly, John, Julie-Anne
Richard, Claire and I, Edward

Julie-Anne with Claire and Helen
Robert with Toby and Sam

Easter 2007

three-seater privy in the garden) so she sold it in 1946 to the Hollicks. Hilaire Hollick had a flair for 'doing up houses' and in 1948, when she had finished Cattespoole, she put it on the market. A lot of prospective buyers were suspicious that the Hollicks had found dry rot and were thus moving on quickly but, as Guy had stayed in the house, he knew it was sound. Not only was it a lovely old Elizabethan house but it also had 100 acres and we thought we had no hope of buying it. Ben succeeded and managed to buy the property at our reserve price of £12,000.

CATTESPOOL

Cattespoole became ours and we spent our whole married life there, with me remaining on after Guy died in December 1984 until I moved away in 2002, after 54 years, when I was in my eighties. Our son, Robert, and his second wife, Jilly, were happy to take on the house and land.

We inherited a tenant farmer called Mr. West; the place was very dishevelled and West a useless farmer. He lived in Cattespoole Cottage at the other end of the farm and spent most of his time in the pub. He had six cows and 12 hens! We eventually evicted him on the grounds of bad husbandry. Guy said "Do you mind if I farm it myself?" with me replying "I thought I had married a doctor, not a farmer". Guy's response was that he had only taken up medicine in order to farm! So in the end I did marry a farmer but Guy kept up with his doctoring and farmed in his 'spare time'. We went through all the vicissitudes of farming: hens, geese, sheep, turkeys, pigs and eventually a successful Friesian dairy herd with a few Jerseys to keep the butter-fat high. The pleasure of skimming the beautiful yellowy cream off the milk the next morning is still with me.

Cattepoole was a fine house to live in but needed a lot of up-keep. We started off married life living with packing cases and orange boxes – at that time these were sturdy wooden crates. We gradually collected up the necessary furniture from house sales and markets. In time we managed to re-roof, put in central heating, replace windows, re-build the chimneys and generally keep it in one piece. This was where the plastering skills I acquired at school came in.

There was not much in the garden apart from a mass of box hedges, an Ophelia rose, a few red peonies and a yew tree outside the privy (to keep away the flies). It was a treat to find the wood filled with snowdrops in our first spring. The garden was a particular joy for both of us, with me concentrating on the shrubs and flowers whilst Guy grew all manner of vegetables and fruit on a large plot. With milk, chickens, eggs and pork we were fairly self-sufficient. We had various people who helped us. At first there were Stefan and Rosie Kiss from Hungary, who were displaced people and lived above the coach house in fairly basic conditions. They were followed, after about a year, by Kurt, a German ex prisoner-of-war who decided to stay in England rather than venture home to what had become East Germany. He worked at a local engineering company and helped on the land at week-ends. He was memorable for his saying "Das dinks ist caput". Lots of things were broken but, somehow, we managed. Kurt lived above the Coach House and finally left us in the mid fifties.

Fred Besley (then aged 15) was working for Mr. West and continued to work at Cattespoole until Guy gave up farming in 1971. Guy really enjoyed breeding pigs. It must have been something to do with their fast procreation time as he could really get into the genetics and see the results fairly quickly. It was all very well having pigs but that meant slurry and that created a great hazard. At least two of our four children nearly drowned in the slurry pits. Rachel was pulled out by her plaits and Michael rescued by the hood of his duffle coat.

There were several other people who came to work on the farm. Cliff and Nancy Geens lived in Cattespoole Cottage. They were followed by John Jerome and then Bill Root. Jack Grinter then became our cow man. He had a cleft palate and a broad Somerset accent; the children all learnt how to swear from Jack! He was an excellent herdsman and when he left in 1971 we sold the herd. Jack lived in Kittenspoole, the cottage we had built just down the lane from Cattespoole; with a view to it being our retirement cottage. The name was a bit corny but memorable! In fact the name Cattespoole has absolutely nothing to do with cats but more to do with a pole used for catching birds. This didn't stop us having lots of cats, Joey being the longest-lived at 19. Horses and dogs were also to feature in our lives.

Guy and I had been married six months when I

said I had to go into Birmingham. Guy wanted to know why and I had to come clean and tell him that I had, in fact, brought my Dachshund, Sandra, back from Austria. She had been in quarantine all this time. Sandra had appeared as a stray when I was in Lendorf and became our pet. If Matron came anywhere near the ward the dog would pop up onto one of the beds and find a hiding place under one of the patients' leg cages. Sandra went on to have many litters of pups and died at a grand old age. Tonka and Sammy were also rather long-lived fellows too. Sammy was a faithful friend to Guy and if we needed to know where Guy was we would find Sammy halfway between the house and Guy. Sammy came on appro from the police pound. He cowered in the corner and Guy said that he was certainly not the dog for us. A day or two later a phone call came to tell us that some cattle had escaped from one of the fields. Guy went out to put them back only to find that Sammy, a half-cross Corgi, had gone ahead of him, rounded them up and sent them back into their proper field. They were forever friends after that incidcnt.

Our first pony arrived in 1952 at the same time as my elderly and dying mother-in-law; both brought down from Yorkshire by horsebox and ambulance respectively. Mother-in-law died shortly after but the pony lived for some years. Dixie was a piebald pony equipped with a basket instead of a saddle; so the children were able to ride on her back before they could even walk. A succession of ponies followed; some more successful than others. All the children learnt to ride and had enormous fun taking part in Pony Club, gymkhanas, hunting and riding over the farm and along the lanes to meet up with friends who also had ponies. Cattespoole was a wonderful place for children to grow up. They had a truly 'free range' childhood. There was always something to do: eggs to collect and sort, stables and tack to clean, vegetables to prepare and bales to collect and stack. It certainly gave them all a great work ethic!

I had help with the children. When Robert was

born in 1949 Margie came to live with us for about a year. After Margie left to get married there began a succession of au-pair girls. The girls always came through personal recommendation from Austria, Germany, Switzerland or Finland. They usually stayed a year and became part of the family. They were good company for me since Guy worked such long hours and I still correspond with some of them all these years later.

Our family holidays were usually taken during the first few weeks of September. We started off by going to Penbryn in Wales and Polzeath in Cornwall; piling the family into our Vanguard estate. Later on we went to other places in Wales: Tenby, Nolton Haven and New Quay – always with the idea that we might find a little holiday house. Finally, in 1964, my friend Betty told us that the cottage on the beach at New Quay was for sale. I had known the cottage when it was a restaurant and loved the position – very close to the beach looking across the bay to the town. We spent many happy years visiting Traeth Gwyn

House. Guy would sometimes dash down after work on a Friday so that he could check how his potato crop was growing or whether the apples were doing their thing.

We knew the house was on unstable ground but somehow we managed to keep it in one piece with constant rebuilding work, especially after an earthquake hit Cardigan Bay on 19th July 1984. Over the years it slipped down the hillside and was getting ever closer to the sea. The walls cracked and the floors became uneven. We finally parted company in 2001 with much sadness, but only after nearly 40 years of wonderful holidays enjoyed by us, our children, our grandchildren and many guests.

In the late 1960's we were really lucky to find a little house on Menorca. Guy needed the warmth and liked to have his own house in the sun as he found travelling to foreign places a bit of a challenge. Being Guy he wasn't very good at sitting still but in Menorca he would, at least, settle down with a book when he wasn't cooking, swimming or painting and repairing the villa. For the family the journey through France to Barcelona in our VW campervan was enormous fun and educational – we chose a different route each time and camped out at night. In Barcelona, our campervan would be swung up in a big net onto the ferry which took us overnight to Menorca.

Both Guy and I were keen skiers and the ski slopes were hard to resist. In the early days we went with friends. At that time there were not many ski lifts, so we would spend most of the day walking uphill with seal skins attached to our skis to get just a couple of good runs down the mountain. Later on we took groups of both our children and their friends to various resorts in Austria which was great fun.

Guy had a coronary in 1965 at the age of 53, so farming became physically more demanding for him and we let out some of the land to a neighbour. In 1981 our eldest son, Robert and his first wife, Cécile, converted the barn behind Cattespoole and came home from London at week-ends. They loved the farm and did many of the maintenance tasks around the place. Although Robert trained as an accountant he became a very successful businessman owning ships and running a shipping line. I remember one of his first entrepreneurial efforts was to bag up manure from the farm and sell that around the district. In the late 80's Robert was able to buy the neighbouring farm and some woods for shooting, thus increasing the acreage to 500.

When, in 1974, a new road was being built between Redditch and Bromsgrove, stone was required and the road builders noticed that we had an old quarry on our land; so they quarried the stone and landscaped the area with a dam and bunds to create a fishing lake. The lake was great fun. There have been only two winters when it has frozen over enabling ice hockey to be played but it was good for swimming and canoeing as well as fishing. Guy's ashes are buried on the island in the lake.

Guy continued to practise surgery, sometimes tormented by angina but with no complaints. After retirement in 1977 he gardened with even more enthusiasm and took all his excess produce to two local W.I. Markets, which became a little like out-patient departments as his customers would turn up each week and ask questions about what the plants should or should not be doing. He stood no nonsense from other members of the stalls – mostly women – and had the place running smoothly and efficiently. Guy also brewed quantities of vermouth (to dose his gin with) and white wine. An additional retirement job for Guy was to serve on Medical Appeals Tribunals.

I had two bouts of cancer in the 80's and 90's but

have hung in there. In my eighties, thinking that I should get 'with it' and learn about computers, I enrolled at the local college. The teacher said what I thought was "Move your mouth". I'm a bit deaf and didn't realise that she was actually saying "Move your mouse". Computers and I parted company but I still wish I could communicate with all my friends via e-mail. I have mastered a fax machine as well as video and DVD players, so I don't feel too left out of the 21st century but I'm not sure that iPods are quite my thing.

BRAVE NEW WORLD?

You would have thought that two major World Wars within 21 years of each other would have taught mankind a thing or two about peace. But no, we just had to carry on fighting. There was great distrust between the USA and Russia before the Second World War, so their 'friendship' during the war was simply the result of having a mutual enemy – Nazi Germany. This distrust was still present at the end of the war, especially after the first Stalin heard about the atom bomb attack on Hiroshima was when news got back to Moscow after the event. The Cold War is the name given to the relationship that developed primarily between the USA and the USSR. The Cold War was to dominate international affairs for decades and many major crises occurred.

In Korea in 1950 what started out as a civil war escalated into a conflict between the capitalist powers of the United States with its allies and the communist powers of the People's Republic of China and the Soviet Union. Heavy casualties were suffered by both sides, with many civilians being caught up in the fighting and destruction. To this day no peace treaty has ever been signed but there is a glimpse of the opening-up of North Korea to outsiders.

In 1956 Hungary revolted against the USSR but was 'put down' in the most brutal fashion with 30,000 people loosing their lives and another 200,000 leaving their homeland. At the same time there was a crisis at the Suez Canal which was nationalised by the Egyptian President, Colonel Nasser. There were many reasons for this happening; not least that Britain and France wanted to keep the canal under their control. British and French troops were sent in whilst Israel, not wanting to be left out, also made their own invasion plans. The joint forces quickly defeated the ill-equipped Egyptians. Egypt reacted by sinking 40 ships in the canal thus blocking all passage. Following international pressure, particularly from the USA, a cease-fire was called. The battle could have become even more bloody as the USSR was sitting on the sidelines waiting to pounce. The rest of the world shunned Britain and France for their actions in the crisis and soon a UN salvage team moved in to clear the canal. Control of the canal was given to Egypt in March 1957 with the proviso that they allowed all vessels of all nations free passage through it. Suez is the only direct means of travel from the Mediterranean to the Indian Ocean making it vital for the flow of trade between Asia, the Middle East, Europe and the USA.

During the 1950's whilst all this was going on I was busy having three more children: Rachel-Claire, born 1953, Julie-Anne, born 1957 and Michael, born in 1959. There were a fair few nappies to wash during these years but we led a happy country life on the farm where children could 'free range'. Cattespoole was rather chilly without central heating – that came later – and there was a lot of mud around the place. I kept up my physiotherapy for a while by giving some anti-natal classes; otherwise it was a matter of keeping the house and garden running smoothly as well as fitting in the all-important tennis and bridge. Living in a rural area, these provided a good way to entertain friends and became very much part of our life. If the weather was bad, we simply moved to the bridge table!

Sadly George VI died in 1952 at the young age of 56. He had come to the throne unexpectedly following the abdication of his brother, Edward VIII, in 1936. George was diffident and suffered from a speech impediment but was greatly helped in his work by his wife, Elizabeth (later the Queen Mother). The King's greatest achievements were during the Second World War, when the Royal family remained for most of the time at Buckingham Palace (the palace was bombed nine times). He visited severely bombed areas of

London and elsewhere in the country, gaining him great popularity. Having served in the navy during the Second World War the King was also anxious to visit his troops whenever possible.

The King's daughter, Elizabeth II, came to the throne aged 25. The Coronation in June 1953 was a time of great rejoicing. Britain was emerging from the post-war period of a weak economic position and deprivation. Many people bought televisions for the first time so that they, and their neighbours, could watch the celebrations; street parties were organised and loyal subjects from all over the country made their way to London to line the streets. On the eve of the Coronation the announcement was made that Edmund Hillary and Tenzing Norgay had become the first people to reach the summit of Mount Everest.

In the 1950's, with the availability of more interesting fabrics, fashion became quite opulent, with corseted waists and swirling skirts to mid-calf. Coco Chanel rather bucked the trend and designed neat suits and dresses which were marvels of simplicity. Menswear had something of an Edwardian feel – with a tight-fitting retro style; originally intended to appeal to the young man about town, it manifested itself in popular fashion as the Teddy boy style.

The decade of the 50's gave birth to a whole new music scene. Jazz already existed; followed by swing, big band and bebop but the new rock-and-roll music which evolved in the USA in the late 1940's and early 1950's was to spread quickly to the rest of the world. Rock-and-roll had an unprecedented social impact influencing lifestyles, fashion, attitudes and language. Amongst the prominent rock-and-roll musicians were: Elvis Presley, Little Richard, Buddy Holly and Chuck Berry. It later spawned the various sub-genres of what is now simply called 'rock music'.

Our children grew up in 'The Sixties' – that period of huge change; some might say for the worse. We certainly knew about the music because they would play it rather loudly and we really could not understand what they saw in the Rolling Stones or the Beatles. We were glad, though, that they did not get caught up in the drug scene which really kicked off during those years and which, today, is a real scourge of society. The 60's was the first time that the young became the leaders of fashion. They were excited by the new designs which were made possible by the invention of nylon, lycra and tights. Clothes were colourful and skirts very short! Gradually the older generation raised their hems and started to wear jolly kipper ties and stopped having their hair permed. Women were no longer restricted to wearing girdles and stockings on a daily basis; jeans became normal wear and women wore trousers more often. Whilst all this was going on men were landing on the moon. Could any of us have imagined this when we were children and looking up into the sky at night?

One of the most significant medical advances of the 20th century occurred in the 1960's. The development of the contraceptive pill played an important role in the women's liberation movement. It enabled women to choose when they wanted their children but it also encouraged promiscuity without the fear of getting pregnant and this, in turn, caused an increase in sexually transmitted disease. Worldwide there are now around 100 million women taking 'the pill'. Other medical advances made during this decade included the introduction of the Polio vaccine in 1955 (which was a real boon), the first organ transplants and the discovery of the double-helical structure of DNA.

In the USA social change was created by the American civil rights movement, the rise of feminism, gay rights and the invention of the microchip. In Africa the 1960's was a period of radical political change as countries gained independence from their European colonial rulers, only for this rule to be replaced in many cases by civil war or corrupt dictatorships. The Berlin Wall was built in 1961, followed a year later by the Cuban Missile Crisis and the Six-

Day War in the Middle East in 1967. All this was overshadowed for ten years from 1965 by the Vietnam War with the USA supporting South Vietnam against communist North Vietnam. Over one million military lives were lost with more than double that number of civilians being killed. It was a savage waste of life with North Vietnam eventually taking Saigon and unifying Vietnam under a communist government.

England had its own problems nearer to home with Northern Ireland. For 30 years from the mid sixties there was public disorder in Northern Ireland. The Protestant Loyalists and the Catholic Republicans murdered, bombed, went on hunger strikes and kidnapped at home and in England. It was a complex period with its roots some time back in the history of Ireland (too complex to explain here). 3,500 people died during 'The Troubles' with many more maimed. It is with great hope that peace is now the order of the day.

The Seventies saw our children growing up into

young adults and pursuing their careers; Robert as an accountant before he graduated to shipping and Rachel-Claire as a teacher, then later on Julie-Anne becoming an account manager for a software house (what is software I ask myself?) and Michael going off to work in Hong Kong for a few years. I was then freed up to spend more time on charity work with the British Red Cross and various local charities. Guy retired so we became busy with W.I. Country Markets selling our excess produce as well as plants especially propagated for sale. We also had to get used to Decimalisation. In 1971 we lost our lovely old pennies, half crowns, sixpences and threepences to have them replaced with new pence and pounds. It took a little time to get used to, but the maths was certainly easier; no more £ s d in three columns. Out went slide rules – in came calculators which made mathematical life less complicated.

After Guy died in 1984 I started travelling again. I was lucky enough to visit Patagonia, Guatemala, the West Indies on a tall ship,

America and India to name but a few. Latterly I have been fortunate enough to spend a month each year in South Africa; leaving behind the cold of England to seek the warmth of friends and climate in Africa. Travelling is now more difficult for me but I can still get to Dublin to see my daughter, Julie-Anne, and her family and to Menorca to top-up with some sun early in the season.

I made a very fortuitous move to Chipping Campden, Gloucestershire, in 2002. I might have left behind my home of 54 years but I have settled into a friendly community where everything is within easy reach. The town is one of the most beautiful in England with so much going on it would be hard to get bored. I no longer play tennis but I do manage to play bridge at least four times a week and more if I can find people to play! I continue to make new friends and have even been known to invite in a passing day tripper for a glass of wine or a coffee. I no longer drive but have 'Archie', my trusty scooter, to charge around town on.

With great interest I now watch the next generation of seven grand children make their way in the world. What will their world be like? Will they see as many changes as I have witnessed? And, above all, will they and their peers manage to bring about a peaceful world I wonder?

FAMILY

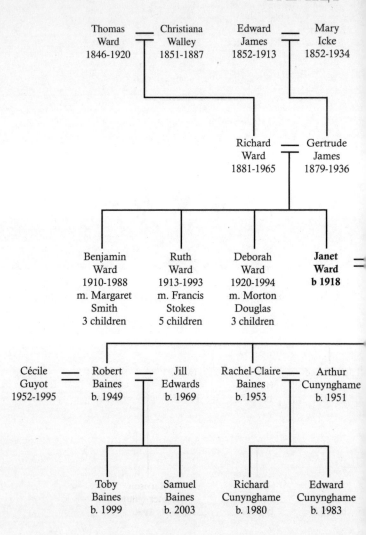

| Thomas
Ward
1846-1920 | — | Christiana
Walley
1851-1887 | Edward
James
1852-1913 | — | Mary
Icke
1852-1934 |

| Richard
Ward
1881-1965 | — | Gertrude
James
1879-1936 |

| Benjamin
Ward
1910-1988
m. Margaret
Smith
3 children | Ruth
Ward
1913-1993
m. Francis
Stokes
5 children | Deborah
Ward
1920-1994
m. Morton
Douglas
3 children | **Janet
Ward
b 1918** — |

| Cécile
Guyot
1952-1995 | — | Robert
Baines
b. 1949 | — | Jill
Edwards
b. 1969 | Rachel-Claire
Baines
b. 1953 | — | Arthur
Cunynghame
b. 1951 |

| Toby
Baines
b. 1999 | Samuel
Baines
b. 2003 | Richard
Cunynghame
b. 1980 | Edward
Cunynghame
b. 1983 |

124

TREE

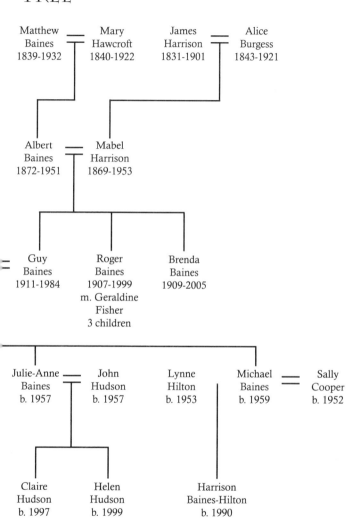

Matthew Baines 1839-1932 — Mary Hawcroft 1840-1922

James Harrison 1831-1901 — Alice Burgess 1843-1921

Albert Baines 1872-1951 — Mabel Harrison 1869-1953

Guy Baines 1911-1984

Roger Baines 1907-1999 m. Geraldine Fisher 3 children

Brenda Baines 1909-2005

Julie-Anne Baines b. 1957 — John Hudson b. 1957

Lynne Hilton b. 1953

Michael Baines b. 1959 — Sally Cooper b. 1952

Claire Hudson b. 1997

Helen Hudson b. 1999

Harrison Baines-Hilton b. 1990

ACKNOWLEDGMENTS

Lino cut prints throughout were all made by
Janet circa 1933 - whilst she was at school.

Photograph of Charterhouse Swimming
Team reproduced by kind permission of the
Governing Body of Charterhouse.

Line drawing of Cattespoole (page 97)
by Honor Gaunt.

Line drawing of Traeth Gwyn (page 105)
by Vera Hankinson.

126

THANKS

I would like to thank:

My mother, in particular, for telling us her story and for reading each chapter as I wrote it, although she did not know that it was destined to become a book.

My late father for writing down a potted history of his life, without which we might not have known so much about his life before marriage.

Various members of our extended family, who each held little pieces of a rather large jigsaw puzzle.

The Internet, which was invaluable for checking facts. I do not promise to have everything correct but this is a storybook not a textbook!

And of course you for buying this book, which will benefit charities supported by my mother.

Rachel-Claire Cunynghame